His Blood, Not Mine

Hellen Jeans

a Passion
for Learning
Discovering new horizons

A Passion for Learning
Kent Enterprise House
The Links
Herne Bay
Kent CT6 7GQ
United Kingdom
www.apassionforlearning.co.uk

ISBN 9781849141185

Cover design: Hellen Jeans
Illustrations: Hellen Jeans
Printed by Lightening Source International, UK

First Edition 2011

For Green Ears,

Thank you so much for helping

me to know His love.

Contents

Acknowledgements

Thank you, Lizzie, for being my true friend. You have taught me so much about God, love and friendship and I truly don't mind when you nag me!

Thank you Tracy for inspiring me, you have given me so much confidence in my writing. I have learnt so much from your teaching and your honesty, there have been times when I have felt unable to move forward but your experiences and guidance have shown me the way.

Thank you, Marilyn, for your confidence in me and for pushing me forward at times in front of the microphone instead of behind the mixing desk. It has been a privilege and honour to share my poetry at your concerts and retreats. Thank you too for being my techie geek friend that actually enjoys talking about gadgets!

Thank you, Fluffy, for your unfailing friendship through good times and bad. You are always at the end of a text so I never feel alone. I watch with pride the small steps you make and l can see the flower waiting to bloom inside.

Thank you, Tony, for bringing me to the Beacon Church and encouraging those first tentative steps.

Thank you, Mel, you welcomed me into your family, held my hand through dark and desperate times and introduced me to our Father God.

Thank you, Sam, you took me under your wing when I was lost, had faith in me and made your home mine.

Thank you John and Jo, Lesley, Kay, my Cell group and my Beacon family, I love you all. You have demonstrated Gods love by the way you have welcomed me without judgement into your fold and you have patiently shown and explained to me God's word, despite my unending questions!

Thank you Gill for being someone I could trust to help me edit this book. You are one of the ways that I know that God had a hand on my life many years ago!

Thank you to all the brothers and sisters I have met during my two years of being a Christian that have nurtured and encouraged me, especially those who I have met with Marilyn and Tracy.

And finally thank you Father God, you adopted me as your child and transformed me with your love. I am yours forevermore.

Foreword

I first met Hellen in Dec 2009 when she attended a Conference that Marilyn Baker and I were leading at Green Pastures Christian Retreat Centre. I felt immediately drawn to her and was glad to have the opportunity to get to know her. As the week progressed, I was moved and challenged by her growing trust in God as her true Daddy. A new Christian, her faith was real and full of a lovely simplicity. Hellen shared a little of her story with the group, she had been through much pain and trauma in her life and was obviously still working through the aftermath. But one thing that really struck me was her hope in God and desire to hear Him and know Him in deeper and deeper ways. Unlike many of us who have been through bad experiences, there was no cloud of bitterness hanging over Hellen. Instead she inspired and encouraged us as she read out the poems and songs she'd started writing since beginning her journey of healing and trust in God. These are the poems and songs you will be reading in this book. They are real, beautiful, soul searching and full of the hope and joy that God our Father loves to give us.

Since that first meeting I have got to know Hellen much more because she is now helping us in our ministry as a sound engineer and driver.

She is a great friend and very gifted in many areas. She has continued writing and her poems and insights have continued to inspire and encourage. Someone suggested to Hellen that she consider making a book of her poems. Where some of us may sit on such a suggestion, waiting for God to open the door, Hellen immediately rose to the challenge and this lovely book is the result!

As someone who has been through traumas in my own life and who is also a writer, I have been deeply inspired both through Hellen's faith and her writing. Her poems touch me in my heart and minister hope and God's love to me. Hellen's refusal to let her experiences crush her and her passion for living her life to the full potential that God has put within her have challenged me, so that I too will try to live and love fully in my life. I count it a real privilege and honour that Hellen has asked me to write the Foreword for her book. I am thrilled to do so and commend it to you with all my heart. I know that as you read it these poems and stories that have come out of her real experiences of life and God, will touch you in your deepest places and you will hear the whisper of your Daddy's voice of love.

Tracy Williamson

MBM Trust

Introduction

My life fell apart when I was raped while living abroad; it also stirred up issues from many years ago. I started self-harming to cope, I have no idea why, I didn't even know anyone who self-harmed. Eventually I came back home in deep distress, under the care of the mental health team, on medication and admitted a number of times to the psychiatric unit. I met a friend on a college course in 2007 and he encouraged me to come to his church - The Beacon Church in Herne Bay. I had never been involved with church before and did not believe in God. But as I went sporadically and came to know the people there I began to see something different. I became a Christian at Easter 2009 and was baptised that September.

My life was starting to change; however, my self-harm was becoming life threatening. But I really started to feel God. I didn't understand love; to me someone who loved you hurt you. My trust had been totally broken. It was hard because I could not see God as a father figure, but I suddenly had a realisation that He really was my Dad and He loved me so much whatever I did. Each time I self-harmed I knew I was hurting Him too and that hurt me even more than the physical pain.

It's been a long hard struggle, but it is over a year since I last hurt myself. My life has now changed completely. The people at church are my family and through their love towards me and unfailing support through such tough and hopeless times, I now truly understand Gods love for me. I feel that love so strongly every day. I know that I was at rock bottom, I could not forgive myself, but He did, and continues to do so every time I feel I fail. His love has changed me. It's been a slow step by step process, but I know He will and is using the things I have gone through to help me grow strong and also to help others.

I started journaling as a way to express my feelings and get the unspeakable out. When I became a Christian this developed into a form of prayer journaling, writing down helpful scriptures and prayers I sometimes read out on a Sunday. One morning I when I woke, it had snowed overnight and I could not go out. I seemed to have words and a tune in my head so I raked out my old piano keyboard and started tapping out some notes and scribbling words down on a scrap of paper with a pencil. I have not learnt music composition so the tunes were very simple but again helped me to express myself. I get words rolling around in my head for days until they suddenly started to come together, often during the middle of the night, so most of my writing is done in bed on my iPod in the dark! I write it down just as it comes, sometimes with little editing so that it is truly from my heart.

After attending some of Tracy Williamsons 'Listening to God' workshops, I started noticing and being prompted by things that I saw in the world around me. It always leads me to a deeper understanding of my relationship with God and so I believe this is one of the ways God is speaking to me.

I have been encouraged by Marilyn Baker to read some of my poems out at her concerts and have also read some of them during Sunday worship at the Beacon Church, people started to approach me to ask for copies of poems and if I would be doing a book of them. It seemed a ridiculous idea but the more I prayed about it, it seemed the right thing to do.

My desire is to reach and touch others in need through my simple words, to bring good from painful times. To help people know the true love of their Father God bringing healing and life.

Hellen Jeans

As for you also, because of and for the sake of the covenant of the Lord with His people, which was sealed with sprinkled covenant blood, I have released and sent forth your imprisoned people out of the waterless pit.   *Zechariah 9 v11 (AMP)*

Part One

Learning to Love

Angels Dance around You

Lizzie is always telling me that "angels are dancing with joy in heaven because of me". This song is my story.

As you wait behind me,
With sadness in your eyes,
Both God and I can see,
The seed of life you hide.

Angels dance around you,
Rejoice you are alive,
They know that you are healing,
And see you grow with pride.

As you walk beside me,
With questions in your eyes,
Both God and I can see,
A fruit forming inside.

As you stand before me,
With hope now in your eyes,
Both God and I can see,
The flowers bursting wide.

As I sing God's praises,
With head now held up high,
Both God and I will be,
Forever side by side.

Loved

This was the very first poem I wrote to express my love for my Father God. I wrote this at Green Pastures, a Christian Retreat centre in Poole. Green Pastures is a special place to me as it was where I first really started to heal. I had been hearing distressing voices for months due to my depression and post-traumatic stress. Towards the end of my week there, I realised my head was quiet - the voices had stopped! I never heard them again. God's love is amazing and the fact that it will never fail is almost too much to comprehend (1 Corinthians 13 v4-8).

I love You so much.
You're the light that took my darkness
    away,
Protecting me through the night and the
    day,
I now want to breathe, be here and stay,
Because You love me so much.

Love never fails.
I didn't know what love was before You
    came along,
I didn't know that You were right and I
    was so wrong,
I was weak but You have made me
    strong,
Because Your love never fails.

A love that lasts forever.
You give me a warmth and peace in my
    heart,
I feel Your arms around me that will
    never ever part,
I know now that was even before my
    first day began to start,
Because it is a love that lasts forever.

Love is patient, love is kind.
It does not envy, it does not boast,
It is not proud. It is not rude,
It is not self-seeking,
It is not easily angered,
It keeps no record of wrongs.
Love does not delight in evil
But rejoices with the truth.
It always protects, always trusts,
Always hopes, always perseveres.
Love never fails

1 Corinthians 13 v4-8

The Hug

I was in the Minor Injuries Unit being treated for my self-harm injuries; lying on a trolley under a blanket I just wanted a hug. I always found it hard to reconnect with God after harming as I felt ashamed and that I had let Him down, but this time I prayed, and asked for a hug. I physically felt a warmth like a duvet wrapped around me and I knew instantly that it was Gods arms holding me tight, giving me that hug I was so desperate for.

I thought I was just all alone,
Until one night I prayed.
Frightened, hurt and on my own,
He came to me and stayed.

I closed my eyes,
And held my breath,
And longed just for a hug.
His warmth filled my heart,
His arms held me tight,
His voice a whisper just for me.

"You are my child,
I chose you,
And you are mine,
I'm always here,
I'll never ever, ever leave you".

That hug it changed what I could see,
I do not fight alone.
My Fathers here beside me,
I just had never known.

"You are my child,
I chose you,
And you are mine,
I'm always here,
I'll never ever, ever leave you".
"I'll never ever, ever leave you".

Love Is a Mystery

I could not understand 'unconditional love'. People who had said they loved me, hurt me. How could I trust 'love'? My cell group helped me understand that it meant doing something for someone without expecting anything in return. God loves me; I don't need to do anything to earn that love. It's unconditional.

Love is a mystery,
It was never explained to me.
Love is a mystery,
My eyes are tightly closed.

Love is all around me,
I didn't know that it was there.
Love is all around me,
My eyes are still closed.

Love is in our friendship,
Yet I do not understand.
Love is in our friendship,
My eyes they cannot see.

Love is a gift from God,
Can this be completely true?
Love is a gift from God,
My eyes begin to see.

Love is everlasting,
I love God and He loves me.
Love is everlasting,
My eyes are open now.
I can truly see. God loves me.

My Precious One

During a session with Tracy at Green Pastures she asked us to listen to God for our true God-given names (Isaiah 62 v2). The name He had revealed to her was "Daughter of Mercy". God knows our name (Isaiah 43 v1) and His name for me is "My precious one".

Listen, listen to my voice my daughter,
To what I say to you my precious one.

In my sight,
Night and day,
Honouring me,
In every single way.

Held, held in my arms my daughter,
You mean everything to me my precious
    one.

Loved, loved forever my daughter,
I love you every day my precious,
    precious one.

The nations will see your righteousness,
And all kings your glory;
You will be called by a new name
That the mouth of the Lord will bestow

Isaiah 62 v2

Lord God Almighty

This song is an expression of the roles that God fulfils in my life. The fact that I am here today is a miracle. I play the trumpet myself and to believe that the angels are singing and trumpets are playing a fanfare because I am here is so amazing. But each one of us is so precious to God and He celebrates us every day.

Lord God Almighty,
Lord God Holy Father,
With me throughout the night and the
    day,
Here by my side and here to stay,
Lord God my Father full of love.

*An angel choir praising glory from
    heaven above,
A trumpet fanfare heralding amazing
    love,
Chosen and precious child of God,
A miracle before you I am this day today.*

Lord God my Saviour,
Lord God my Counsellor,
New path begun walking hand in hand,
Guided through darkness here I stand,
Lord God my Father full of love.

Lord God my Healer,
Lord God the Conqueror,
Battling with me against enemies,
Healing the scars of histories,
Lord God my Father full of love.

24

Lord God my Creator,
Lord God King Eternal,
Plans that He's got in store for me,
Just have to listen, wait and see,
Lord God my Father full of love.

Coming Home

During an MBM conference learning about Zephaniah 3 v14-17, I was so touched and deeply wanted to feel Gods love. I felt in the midst of deep, dark struggles. I was lost and feeling ashamed that I did not want to be the woman God had created me as. But coming home meant I must belong there, that it was my home. God wanted me as His Daughter in His home. I just needed to make the journey and would be safe, finally at home.

If the enemy holds you tight,
And you're punished day by day,
You feel lost for all eternity,
A disappointment in every way.

But you're coming home to Me.
Yes you're coming home to Me.
I rejoice over you with singing,
For I take great delight in you.

But the Lord your God has saved you,
And He loves you day by day,
He gathers you, brings you back to Him,
Will all your sins paid in every way.

And you'll never fear harm again,
Praised and honoured day by day,
Be glad and rejoice with all your heart,
Now He's your Father in every way.

At that time I will gather you;
At that time I will bring you home.
Zephaniah 3 v20

Love Is the Food of Life

During communion at church, Maggie spoke about how the bread and wine being the body and blood of Christ is our food, our spiritual nutrition (John 6 v35). If God is love then love is our food that gives us life. All that we need comes from God.

God He moves within us,
Marching forth each day.
He gives us energy,
And breathes in life,
Through the body and blood of Christ.
God He moves within us,
In every way.

*Love it is the food of life,
It feeds my heart and soul,
Love it is the food of life,
Because God loves you and me.*

God He grows within us,
Listens when we pray.
He gives us freedom,
From our past life,
Through the body and blood of Christ.
God He grows within us,
In every way.

27

There Is a Rock

*Someone said to me "you don't know what the rock is
that you are standing on until you reach rock bottom".
This is so true, I had truly reached rock bottom before I
became a Christian. I did not believe in God. But
something, someone was stopping me from going that
one step too far. I could feel arms holding me up and
they were the arms of God. I did not have the strength
on my own to survive, but God gave me that strength.
He is my Rock.*

> *There is a rock I stand on,*
> *It will never go away,*
> *I always know that it is there,*
> *With trust I rest today.*

Every time I fall right down,
It's a pillow night and day,
When the darkness is all around,
A light house shines my way.

With my faith I trust my feet,
I just close my eyes and pray,
My loving hugging friend forever,
This rock is here to stay.

When I think I'm all alone,
With a whisper He will say,
"I never will abandon you,
With Me you'll always lay".

Just As I Am

Having believed I had lost my virginity to rape, I saw myself as impure and unclean. However, the definition of purity includes 'freedom from guilt or evil' and as the responsibility for being raped lies solely with the person who chose to hurt you then they are the only ones who can be considered to be impure. Deuteronomy 22 v25-26 shows that God does not see rape as sex but as a crime and no sin has been committed by the woman who has been raped. Isaiah 62 v1-5 inspired this song, this is how God sees me, I have done nothing wrong, He loves me just as I am.

> *Just as I am,*
> *I'll always be,*
> *Just as I am,*
> *Beauty to You.*

A beautiful crown,
In the hand of my God,
No longer forsaken,
I'm named now anew,
'My delight is in you'.

Owned and protected,
A virgin white as snow,
Married to You my Lord,
A bright burning torch,
Shining glory for You.

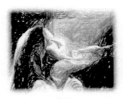

29

Part Two

You Are My Child

Beautiful

I had just climbed up onto Dartmoor; the view was stunning as I sat on a rock to catch my breath. I sent this as a text to friends because although I do not feel beautiful, that is not how God sees me.

God made heaven, the Earth, you and
  me.
All of this is Gods world,
Beauty that he can see.
Despite what we may think we're like,
God sees what is within us.
And it's the image of Christ that is what
  we'll be.

My Precious Child

Staying overnight at a pastors house after doing a concert with Marilyn and Tracy, I found myself awake in the night needing to write down the words that I knew God wanted to say to the pastor. He had spoken to us of how felt he had failed God and I just wanted to let him know in my simple understanding how precious he really was.

My precious child,
How much I love you,
You mean everything to me,
You are my creation,
And I'll be with you,
Until beyond eternity.

My son has died for you,
That's how special you are,
Now listen and trust in me,
There are many plans,
I still have for you,
That you will honour so faithfully.

I know every thought,
Before you think it,
You will never fail to me,
You are forgiven,
No matter what you do,
The blood of Jesus sets you free.

So still I love you,
For every breath you take,
You live your life for me,
And when you feel,
That very deep despair,
Just pray and be with me.

I'd Rather Be in Heaven

Sometimes it's hard to be alive. I have felt suicidal in the past when the pain seemed too much to bear. Now I know God I don't want to die anymore; but when the world around just seems to hurt me more and more I find the thought of being in heaven with Jesus a much safer place to be. However, God has a purpose for me, and I need to be alive for that. He will keep me safe.

I sometimes think that heaven,
Is a place I'd rather be.
I want to be there with Jesus,
And feel completely free.

Because it's so hard to live with pain
    inside,
To feel so very broken.
All the memories that fill my head,
Are powerful and unspoken.

So the world seems unsafe and dark,
There is no place to hide.
Who is there I can really trust,
Is God really at my side?

But now the answers coming clear and
    strong,
Love envelops me today.
The Lord my God is with me,
And will always show the way.

The hope I never thought I'd have,
The reason to be alive.
And as I know that you created me,
I have a purpose to survive.

So here I am today,
Your precious one.
Your love my faith, a hope,
God let your will be done.

You Give Me Strength

I self-harmed for many years. It served many functions, but was mainly a way of coping with my emotions and painful memories. I now have not cut myself for over a year. Why? Because I do not need to. Jesus Christ died on the cross for me, He gave His precious blood for me, the scars on His hands and feet replace my scars. His blood, not mine.

You give me strength oh Lord.
My heart and soul are powered by Your
    true love.
Your Holy Spirit runs through all my
    veins,
A life force flowing to every single cell
    within.
Your Son died for me,
His blood spilt for me,
From that blood so precious, so sacred, I
    am now free.
Lord I love you,
My true Father, my King.
Let me be faithful, and know that you're
    here with me now.
So small, so insignificant am I, but yet
    You still chose me to save!

And now it's my turn, to spread the joy
    of knowing Your heart.
To pray, to love and to hug a precious
    one.
So that they may too know, of Your true
    love, and a child of God they will then
    surely become.
Oh my Father there is none like You,
I so love You,
I am Yours,
Let me serve You, my only one.

The Walls Were Thick

I woke with a vivid picture of thick, high imposing castle walls, built to protect those inside. The walls I had built up around myself had not protected me though. I had fallen to rock bottom, but something was preventing me from taking that last final step from life. Someone amazing, awesome and holding me tight. Maybe there was hope after all?

The Walls were thick,
And the battlements high.
The drawbridge was up,
And the moat ever so wide.
I was safe inside or so I thought,
All problems locked deep in the dungeon.

But the enemy found a way into my fortress,
I am still not sure how he did.
The dungeon door burst wide open,
And Life seemed to fall all around.
My defences were smashed,
And the world now felt at an end.

So the blood flowed thick and scarlet red.
Pain numbing all other pain.
My life force was fading,
The meds and doctors no help,
My friends were not to be found.
No further was there left to fall down.

But at rock bottom I found myself held,
By whom I did not yet know.
Surely No one could help me right now!
But there were those arms,
Just holding me tight,
And a quiet voice I could hear in my ear:

"You are precious my child".
"I think not!" I replied.
Could this really be true?
"Because I am your Father" I heard,
But how could this be?
No love ever came from this name.

But He is so different,
He has taught me true love,
And I am adopted into His fold.
My life born again,
A new hope I have found,
A purpose my God planned for me.

And so I am here,
With a family I love,
A child of God for always.
I worship out loud,
I pray in the quiet,
My Father right there at my side.

"So why do I write this?"
You must be asking yourself!
Well it's because, if you do not know
That you are loved by God too,
Just ask that He forgive you,
And be born, as His child anew.

I Reach Up My Hand

On the Isle of Wight, Tracy shared a picture of a young child with his mum at the beach. Although the sea is huge and could be scary he was holding onto his mums hand and felt secure to explore the waves. I love to support others but I realise now that I need to let them support me too - to be wise in my trust but to trust, especially in God.

Father God I reach up my hand and
trust in you.

Learning to have that trust has not been
easy,
A small word but such a big thing to do.
When trust has been broken over and
over.
When trust has caused pain and
hardship.
But Trusting in You Lord is a whole
different thing,
You will never break the trust I now
have in You.

I may not understand everything You
have planned for me,
But that is where the trust must be.
As I do not need to understand for You
do,
To hand that over starts to set me free.
You already know why I feel how I feel,
And now I must look to You, to trust
that You know the way.

My destiny lays with You my Father,
My provision is with You and always
   has been,
Even when fear has gripped me that
   You have left and I am alone,
But You never have and never will and I
   praise You!

That fear was because I did not trust.
So now I reach up my hand and trust
   You my God.
Trust that Your strong hand is always
   there and will take my hand in its
   palm.
Your hand will support and guide me
   when I cannot see.

Worry and anxiety can now leave me as
   I know I am safe holding onto You.
Even when it is dark and fear is looming
   I still know,
That when I reach up You are there.
The Light that comes from You Lord
   transforms darkness into sunshine.
You lead me along the path I must
   follow.
And I trust that You know the way.

So I reach up and hold onto Your hand,
Safe and secure in my Father's arms.
Held by a love for all eternity,
Your child and Your creation,
Lord I trust and hold onto You.

I Lift My Eyes

Psalm 121 has always been special to me as it was the first part of the Bible that really spoke to me and opened my eyes to see the words there for me

I lift my eyes to You my Lord, my God,
   my King.
I praise Your name for You have saved
   me,
From sin, despair and unbearable pain,
So all that I am to You I now bring.

It was in the jaws of death I came to
   know You,
When hope and salvation felt lost
   forever,
Your hand reached down, took me in its
   palm and lifted me to Your heart,
And that desperate prayer for a hug
   came true.

Now my strength can only come from
   You Lord,
A miracle I stand here right now,
You chose me as Your daughter to love,
Why I still do not understand, but I
   know that you are now my shield and
   sword.

Though the path is still rocky and the
    hills sometimes steep,
If I follow in Your footsteps I will not
    stumble and fall.
Because You protect me from all evil,
And in Your loving arms, with a new
    found peace deep within me,
I now can rest and sleep.

I lift my eyes to the hills –
Where does my help come from?
My help comes from the Lord,
The Maker of heaven and earth.
He will not let your foot slip –
He who watches over you will not slumber;
Indeed, He who watches over Israel
Will neither slumber or sleep.
The Lord watches over you –
The Lord is your shade at your right hand;
The sun will not harm you by day,
Nor the moon by night.
The Lord will keep you from all harm –
He will watch over your life;
The Lord will watch over your coming and going
Both now and forevermore.

Psalm 121

Rest in Me

I felt deeply ashamed. So ashamed I could not tell even my closest friends. It hurt so much; a physical pain I could feel deep inside my chest, the pain of memories from the past. I know now that I have nothing to be ashamed of, it's not my guilt to carry and I am not to blame. But I could only understand this by talking to close friends, by crying the tears locked away for so long, knowing that I can trust God for all that I need to get me through this and beyond.

Father God please help me,
To rest my weary mind.
The hurt that is within me,
So very deep inside.
Seems to pull all my very being,
To that dark place in which it hides.

I feel ashamed to even tell,
The people that care so much for me.
The feeling that it's all my fault,
So strong inside my mind.
When I finally talk the tears do come,
Pain locked away forever reappears.

But You are my Father,
And I must trust You.
You sent your son,
To take away my sin.
And I must hand over these feelings,
Of guilt and blame to You.

So now I lay in bed exhausted,
It's in Your arms I snuggle down.
Your loving warmth surrounds me,
I rest and close my eyes assured,
You will protect me asleep,
When my guard is surely down.

A daughter of the King,
Is what I am now.
And a precious one at that.
I have been saved,
By Your amazing sacrifice,
Washed clean in robes of White.

And so I must honour that gift,
With all my heart and soul.
To love and be loved by You.
And know with peace that
Tomorrow is a new creation,
Planned by You for me to do.

When the Night Seems Long

Night is when I can feel vulnerable and alone. It feels like I can't protect myself during these dark hours. But if I am lying awake struggling with pictures and thoughts or been woken from a bad dream, I now bring my thoughts to God, my Father and Protector and remind myself that I am not and never will be alone.

When the night seems long and will
    never end,
It easy to feel so very alone.
In Those moments of sadness and falling
    right down,
It's easy to think that hope is far out of
    reach.
When plans keep going wrong and the
    futures not so bright,
It's easy to assume a failure is all that
    you can be.

But Listen and trust is what my God
Says to me.
For I am by your side all through the
    night and you will never be alone
    again.
I am the rock that holds you from falling
    and hope is what you now have.

Your plans are mine and I created your
    future so do not ever feel that you
    have failed.
My precious child how much I love you,
You are everything I want you to be.
So have faith to pray, to love and be
    with me for eternity.

Who Am I?

We all have so many labels; I started listing those I could think of that could be applied to me. Do they really define me? Is that who I am? Maybe, but not to God. To Him I am precious beyond measure, above all other Earthly labels.

Who am I?
A daughter?
A sister?
A friend?

Who am I?
A victim?
A secret?
A child?

Who am I?
A patient?
A client?
A file?

Who am I?
A failure?
A burden?
A waste?

Who am I?
A survivor?
A hope?
A live?

Who am I?
I am a new creation!
I am a miracle!
I am a precious, precious child of God!

Part Three

Listening to God

Sand without Blemish

Walking Marilyn's guide dog Pennie one morning with Tracy in Cromer, we went down onto the beach as the tide was just going out. No-one had yet walked on the sand and it was completely smooth, untouched.

The tide has gone out,
The sand is wiped clean,
Smooth without blemish.

I wake every morning the same.
Jesus died on the cross.
His blood washes my sins clean.
Every day is a fresh.
A new day to try to be like Jesus,
    without sin.
But I am human and cannot be like
    that.
But He does not care,
He will wash me clean each night.

I wake every morning with the tide gone
    out,
Sand without blemish.

The Setting Sun

Away for a break with Marilyn and Tracy, I drove back to their home in the evening. There was a brilliant sunset, but the sky was half hidden under thick black cloud. Somehow, instead of smothering the light, it reflected and made the colours of the sunset even more vivid and intense.

The orange glow of the sun reflects off the gloomy dark clouds as it sets.
The clouds seem to be trying to smother the light but only succeed in making it a deeper more powerful colour.

To fight against the darkness by reflecting the light that is already there, multiplying it tenfold seems a wondrous thing that nature achieves so easily.
To do it myself though seems a far harder thing to do when I feel so overwhelmed by darkness.
But I hear a voice in my ear saying "trust in Me, My light is within you and reflects from you and will ward off even the deepest gloom if you reveal it"

The smallest glimmer of light is reflected and multiplied tenfold by the clouds to defeat the darkness.

If I have faith that He is within me, I can never be defeated, but I have to let Him shine.

The Night Sky

Coming out of a Christmas concert it was a cold frosty night and the stars seemed especially bright. I always find the concept of the universe awesome and it makes me feel very small, but I now understand that it's all part of God's creation, and I am just as an important part of that creation too.

The air is crisp and the night sky clear.
Into the dark inky blackness,
I peer hard and start to focus.
I see the stars begin to twinkle,
Specks of light so far away,
Distant suns reaching out with a fire no
man can recreate.

Only God can create such power, such
beauty.
But he can transform us too,
From a faraway twinkle into a light the
whole world can see.
Just as a bright star guided the wise
men to Jesus,
Our shining light can guide others to
His salvation too.

Those who are lost, lonely and hurting,
Can find a love like no other love,
A love not distant like the stars in the
  night sky,
But here on earth deep inside each of us.
Unlike those distant suns whose fire will
  one day fail,
This love will burn for all eternity.

As I stand and gaze into the night sky,
In awe of these distant constellations,
I feel small, insignificant,
But a strong hand comes beneath me,
  lifting me high,
For to my Father God I am significant.
I may not be a king,
But I am His daughter,
Whom He named 'My precious one'.

Stains of Blood

One morning I put on a pair of jeans I had not worn for a while, they were clean but I noticed the faint self-harmbloodstains that remained stubborn even after repeated washing. I started to think about my stains, would I ever be clean? Isaiah 1 v18 tells us that if we are obedient we shall be washed clean.

Stains of blood,
Are soaked so deep,
Marks of time gone by,
Never to be removed.

Stains of sin,
That have darkened me,
Causing fear, pain and tears,
Are they mine forever?

But a sacred blood,
The blood from Christ,
Washes me so clean,
All sins now gone for good.

I'm white as snow,
No more a blemish,
That's how my God sees me,
I'm forgiven, renewed and clean.

A new stain that falls,
May try to take,
But quickly slips away,

As His shield protects forever.

For I am His,
And He is mine,
His arms now hold me tight.
The Father and His child,
Together now eternally.

*"Come now, let us reason together," says
the Lord.
"Though your sins are like scarlet, they
shall be as white as snow;
Though they are red as crimson, they
shall be like wool.
If you are willing and obedient, you will
eat the best from the land.*

Isaiah 1 v18

Jesus Is Like the Snow

There had been heavy snow during the night. Still in bed the light creeping round the curtains was brighter than normal and there was little sound outside as few cars had ventured out. Under the microscope a snowflake has amazing beauty, each one with its own individual pattern of delicate crystals. These fragile flakes had gently settled everywhere, building up quietly overnight into a thick blanket enveloping the world.

I think Jesus can be like the snow.

Snow falls quietly in the night,
It covers the earth in a blanket, enveloping everything.
You realise it's there in the morning,
The world seems lighter, brighter somehow.
Sun reflects off the snow crystals,
Revealing beauty in something as plain as water.
Snow seems to affect our whole life as we change our day around it.

So how is snow like Jesus?

Jesus can come quietly too in the night,
Protecting with the blanket of His loving
arms, enveloping me.
I know He is there in the morning when
I wake,
My world is lighter, brighter,
The light of Jesus reflects from me,
Bringing beauty to something plain,
showing the life that is now within
me.
My whole life is changed as I strive to
live through Jesus,
To be the person my God created me to
be.
I am here today but will not be gone like
the snow tomorrow.
I live because of Him.

Healing Hands of God

I woke in the morning with a picture in my mind of being held in large strong cupped hands, I felt I had to trust those hands for my healing.

Healing hands of god,
Hands so strong,
Reach down to me
And take me in their palm.
I rest, secure and protected in,
Those healing hands of God.

From the darkness a hand reaches down to me,
I look, startled, I am on my own,
Who could this be?
I reach up hesitantly.

As my hand connects,
Warmth surges through me,
Feeling alive for the first time,
What is this I ask?
This awesome power.

I look up to see,
A miracle appear,
A Father full of love,
Could this love be mine?
A love eternal, true.

For He is mighty,
The King of Kings,
His gift was His son,
How can this be?
Sacred Blood shed for me.

But He does love me,
This I surely know,
A love that heals,
A love that's pure,
An eternal warmth within.

Hands so strong,
Reach down to me,
And take me in their palm.
I rest, secure and protected in
Those healing hands of God,
In whom I love and trust.

The Vine Twists and Winds

Whilst walking in the woods with Lizzie at New Year,
some ivy vines caught my eye. It was a mass of chaos,
going nowhere, but in the middle a number of vines had
met and wound round each other to climb up towards
the tree. To me that reinforced the fact that although
we can exist alone, together with our Christian family
we can be so much more.

The vine twists and winds,
It looks random,
A chaotic growth without purpose,
Seeking but not finding.

But there in the centre,
A pattern appears,
The vines join and twist together,
Growing now as one.

The vine is now stronger,
United with one purpose,
It winds up towards the sky,
Seeking the tall tree.

For the tree gives it life,
A resting place,
The vine will become Secure,
Embracing the trees strength.

Alone life seems without meaning,
But we're not alone,
God's family unites us as one,
Seeking His grace.

He is our tall tree,
Our dwelling place,
With The strength to hold us tight,
Forgiven and secure.

Together we have a purpose,
Together we are strong,
Together we're His children,
Together we belong.

The Blustering Wind

It had been a really windy few days, lying in bed all I could hear was the wind blowing outside. It's amazing how we don't think of the air around us until it becomes fierce and strong, until you can see the effects on the things around us. Without the air we would perish, but even though we cannot see or feel it, we know it's there. Without God I would perish, I cannot physically see or touch Him, but I know He is there. As a scientist I want to see the evidence, the proof to believe. I am that evidence, that proof. I breathe Him every day.

The wind blows and blusters,
It whistles through the cracks,
Leaves blow and swirl,
The trees stripped bare.

The wind blows and blusters,
It's strength so sudden, so sure,
Where's this strength from?
Air we can't see, alive.

The wind blows and blusters,
It whistles through my soul,
Blowing all doubts away,
Clearing my weary mind.

The wind blows and blusters,
Its purpose not always clear,
But God knows His creation,
Just as He knows me.

The wind blows and blusters,
But I feel strangely calm,
My faith will not be blown away,
I am just as strong as the wind,
Your strength now mine.

A Simple Snowdrop

The first bulb to flower in my garden this spring was a single solitary snowdrop. It is such a small simple flower but when I saw it I knew spring had arrived! It can be easy to just feel the pain that can lurk deep inside, but I am more than that now. I know some people look at me and all they see are the scars on my arms, not able to understand the pain that resulted in such self-harm. But I want to be seen as more than scars. I want to radiate Gods light so much that that is all people are able to see. The joy that I am a child of God.

> The first snowdrop holds its head up high,
> Proud to announce the coming spring.
> It may have felt forgotten during those long dark months,
> But it was kept strong and safe while it slept,
> Waiting for that first warmth of the sun to awaken.
> A simple flower,
> Needing no bold colours,
> Heralding the seasons change.

I wonder if I was a flower what would I
herald?
Will people see me and think of sadness
or of joy?
The outer scars or the inner light?
Just another flower or a bloom from
God?
Can I be someone who will herald the
coming of Jesus?
Be proud to hold my head up high?

I have been kept safe through darkened
days by Gods love.
I am proud to be His.
I will hold my head high.
I will announce His coming.
A simple white flower for all to see.

Conclusion

I put together this book of poems to show my healing journey with God so far. Many are just as they come so I hope this encourages you to start writing if you have not already done so – no expertise needed! It's a personal communication with God, He knows you already so just talk to Him. I do not yet know lots of biblical words and am discovering new parts of the Bible every day. People seem to tackle reading the Bible in many ways, for me it's usually as I come across a reference that leads me to a passage I then read, often the whole chapter or even book. I am lucky to have many people around me with more experience of reading the Bible that are able to point the way when needed. I also find looking at different translations helpful too. Sometimes a slightly different wording helps my understanding and enables me to relate it to my life, so I often look up a verse in the New International Version, the Amplified Bible and the Message.

I often feel my understanding of God is childlike but I think that's ok, after all I am His child and He just wants to love me. Although I have had some terrible experiences that no one should have to go through, Jesus experienced more pain than I ever have or will and He is in there with me every step of the way. Jesus gave His precious Holy blood for me. God sacrificed His only Son for me. I do not need to hurt myself anymore; I am worth more than that. His blood, not mine.

As for the future I never thought I'd have? God has His plans for me, I am not sure exactly what they are yet, although He keeps giving me hints and opening doors! I can't wait to find out more!

Trust in Him for your healing, you cannot do it alone just as I couldn't. He desperately wants you to know His Fathers love for you, to forgive you, to be the strength of your heart. Let Him in and He will shine from within you for all the world to see.

Resources

Flying Free With God, Tracy Williamson (New Wine Press)

God Knows My Name, Beth Redman (David Cook)

Crying Scarlet Tears, Sophie Scott (Monarch Books)

Recovery Devotional Bible, New International Version. Ed. Verne Becker (Zondervan)

The Everyday Life Bible (Amplified), with commentary by Joyce Meyer (Faith Words)

The Message Remix: the Bible in contemporary language, Eugene Peterson (NavPress)

MBM – a dynamic itinerant ministry of music, teaching and prayer from Marilyn Baker and Tracy Williamson.
PO Box 393, Tonbridge, Kent TN9 9AY.
Tel: 01732 850855
http://www.mbm-ministries.org
Email: info@mbm-ministries.org
Prayer and information line: 0800 0193709

Firstsigns – A user led voluntary organisation to raise awareness about self-injury and help people who rely on self-injury by providing a safe, friendly message board, ideas for distraction techniques and by inspiring/empowering them to find alternative, healthier coping mechanisms.
http://www.firstsigns.org.uk
Email: info@firstsigns.org.uk

Green Pastures – A Christian retreat and renewal centre.
17 Burton Road, Poole, Dorset BH13 6DT
Tel: 01202 764776
http://www.greenpastures17.wordpress.com
Email: info@green-pastures.org

The Beacon Church Herne Bay
78 Sea Street, Herne bay, Kent CT6 8QE
http://www.beaconhernebay.org.uk

Love Never Fails (from the album *What if We*),
Brandon Heath (Reunion Records)
http://www.brandonheath.net

You are my God (from the album *Everlasting God*),
Brenton Brown (Survivor Records)
http://www.brentonbrown.com

I will change your name (by D.J. Butler) (from the album *From the Beginning*) Marilyn Baker
(Authentic Media)
http://www.mbm-ministries.org

Image Of (from the album *Dream*), Michelle
Tumes (Sparrow Records)

Beauty from Ashes (from the album *All That I Am*), Marilyn Baker (Authentic Media)
http://www.mbm-ministries.org

God is the Strength of my Heart (from the album *God is Good*), Don Moen (Integrity Media).
http://www.donmoen.com

Lightning Source UK Ltd.
Milton Keynes UK
178663UK00002B/119/P